CUMBRIA LIBRARY SERVICES

COUNTY COUNCIL

This book is due to be returned on or before the last date above. It may be renewed by personal application, post or telephone, if not in demand.

C.L.18

Family Life in Britain

1900–1950

Family Life in Britain
1900–1950

Edmund Swinglehurst

A Time Warner Book

This first edition published in 2005

Copyright © Omnipress Ltd 2005

ISBN 0-316-73034-3

Produced by Omnipress, Eastbourne

Printed in Singapore

Time Warner Books
An imprint of
Time Warner Book Group UK
Brettenham House
Lancaster Place
London WC2E 7EN

Photo credits: Mary Evans Picture Library, Mirrorpix and Corbis

Contents

INTRODUCTION 7

1   THE EDWARDIAN YEARS 13

2   THE SCHOOL YEARS 27

3   AT THE SEASIDE 41

4   WORLD WAR ONE 53

5   BETWEEN THE WARS 65

6   WORLD WAR TWO 77

7   POST WAR BRITAIN 93

8   MEMORIES SAVED FOREVER 111

Introduction

When Queen Victoria died and Edward VII became king, the dawn of a new life began to seep through the curtained windows of family homes in Britain. The new day that was beginning was hardly perceptible at first but half a century later it was blazing with a brilliant noon day light that was flooding into every corner of family life.

The change was a psychological one, of a people who had been submerged in a system of social controls by church, education and state and were being impelled towards change by the new circumstances of their lives. The established Victorian way of life had created the national culture of the most powerful nation in the world but had subdued the desire for individual liberty, which now began to grow stronger than the spirit of community and national pride.

The embryonic spirit sprang from the natural vitality of the people and the ingenuity of a few who gave the people's feeling a voice and crystallised their desires. Liberty, equality, fraternity, the results of a revolution which most British people deplored, were at the root of the message which had already been voiced by thinkers like John Stuart Mill and the popular movement of the Chartists who sought not revolution but fair play and better conditions.

LEFT: *FAMILY GROUP*
Papa, Mama and their nine children proudly display their belief in the mission to go forth and multiply, 1900 ⌇

RIGHT: *NANNY IN PARK*
Nanny taking a stroll through Hyde Park in the 1920s with Father and his children. The high class pram, the smart white horse, and expensive riding gear of the little girl reveal the social status of this family ⌇

LEFT: *EDWARDIAN MOTHER*
An Edwardian mother and her two daughters all smartly turned out, as was expected of middle class families ❧

BELOW: *FAMILY IN DRIVEWAY WITH THEIR FORD, 1952*
A model nuclear family stands proudly before the American style Ford 4-door saloon parked in their driveway ❧

By 1900 the new spirit was well established and winning new adherents, though the achievements at first were slight. The availability of new reading matter, including the popular press, increased the fund of public information, which also grew through the increasing ease and accessibility of travel throughout the nation. The railway network, which had been stretching out its tentacles to every part of the kingdom, had enabled ordinary people to become acquainted with their fellow Britons and to develop a sense of personal identity. It also made leisure, until then a privilege of the affluent, available to all through cheap railway excursions such as those offered by a Leicester printer and Temperance worker Thomas Cook. Cook arranged cheap fares to cathedral cities and the seaside as an alternative to drowning misery by excessive drinking.

These forces changed the nature of family life, which had remained undisturbed throughout the Victorian era, and led to an open challenge to the hitherto invulnerable male father figure. They encouraged public expression of

ABOVE: *CHARLES DARWIN (1809–1882)*
The British naturalist, whose theory of natural selection altered the world's opinions about the evolution of living things and caused a national furore. This portrait by J. Cameron shows him in his later years ❧

RIGHT: *KARL MARX (1818–1883)*
The man whose work Das Kapital *was the foundation stone of the Communist ideology which he launched with Frederick Engels as a political manifesto* ❧

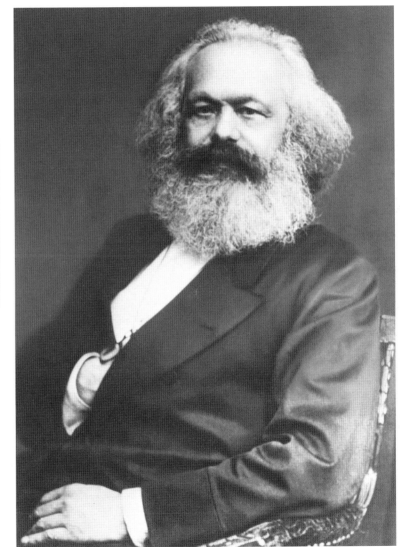

opinions about greviously taboo matters such as the ambitions of Empire, money, religion, and new, disruptive, scientific notions such as those of Charles Darwin and Karl Marx, though matters relating to the male and female sex were strictly avoided.

Other forces were taking up the struggle, among them writers like Bernard Shaw whose radical work included *The Devil's Disciple*, one of three plays for Puritans, H. G. Wells (*The Time Machine*) and Oscar Wilde whose views were challenging the existing complacent ethos reflected in the works of Rider Haggard's imperial hero, *Alan Quartermain* and JM. Barrie's *Peter Pan*. The Great War was a hiatus in the development of the new society, as male members joined the Forces and females of the middle classes volunteered for social work or as nurses in hospitals, while working class women took the place of men in factories producing armaments and other essential equipment.

Once peace had been established the new ideas proliferated among younger members of families. Through wide

BELOW: *BATHING BABIES*
Nurses bathing newborn babies at St Bartholomew's Hospital in London. This famous teaching hospital trained young women in all branches of paediatrics, as well as other medical disciplines &

LEFT: *WOMEN FACTORY WORKERS ICE BISCUITS*
These women are covering biscuits in different colours of sugar icing at the factory of W. R. Jacobs & Co in Liverpool, where mass production systems were in use in 1926

sections of society, the opportunities of a better life in Britain beckoned through the discoveries and inventions of innovative people. Women under the leadership of Emmeline Pankhurst fought for the right to vote and to work. The flight of a Frenchman across the English Channel fired the imagination, as did the appearance of electric trams and motor buses in London and the first popular motor car made by Henry Ford. Ford's invention became a source of much contention in middle class families, while the invention of the safety bicycle provided a vehicle of escape for the masses trapped in grimy towns and cities.

Though many of the new fangled inventions met with resistance, even among those who could afford them,

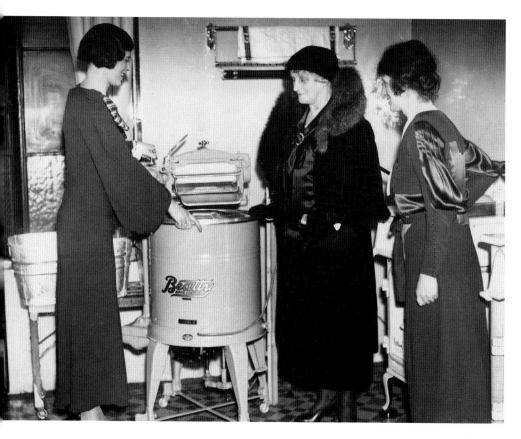

ABOVE: *LADY MOIR OPENS SCHOOL OF ELECTRICAL DOMESTIC SCIENCE*
The president of the Association for Women and Miss Minoprio, principal of the London School of Electrical Science, inspect a combined washing machine and mangle at the school's official opening in Knightsbridge, London, 1934 ꙮ

their evident usefulness as labour saving devices increased their popularity and brought prices down to levels affordable by ever more families. From now on every home in Britain aspired to, or owned, a vacuum cleaner, a washing machine, a refrigerator and sundry items such as food mixers.

In the period between the wars family entertainment was also undergoing a radical change, as evenings spent playing cards and board games or listening to impromptu concerts given by friends began to disappear, as the BBC began regular broadcasts of drama, news and popular music. Such facilities were not enough to keep young members of the family at home however, for the availability of popular *palais de danse*, coffee bars and cinemas made them social centres where the young could indulge in their fashions, changing their hairstyles from bob, to shingle, to Veronica Lake styles. Their dance routines also changed from the foxtrot, tango and Charleston, to jitterbugging, swing and jive without raising parental eyebrows. The new freedom for youth was infectious and led in mid- century to the end of family life as it was once understood.

At first the older members of families were shocked and anxious at the new iconoclastic trends, but becoming accustomed to their own freedom from routine family chores and rituals they, too, began to enjoy a second youth with evening outings, holidays abroad and a more knowledgeable sex life, fostered by the writings of Dr. Emily Stopes, often in competition with their children rather than as guides and mentors.

By the 1950s Britain was on the threshold of a new society and way of life, inconceivable in the days of Queen Victoria, which would turn the nation from the greatest imperial and industrial power on earth into a democracy with high standards of living and freedom envied by all.

SECTION ONE

The Edwardian Years

Edward VII's reign was short – he succeeded his mother Queen Victoria in January 1901 and died in 1910 – but the changes that made 20th century Britain a very different country from that of the 19th century took root during this period.

As Prince of Wales, Edward had gained the reputation of a *bon viveur*. Despite having a beautiful wife, he had many exotic lady friends such as the actress Lily Langtry, owned a string of race horses including Derby winners, and showed a preference for the racy life of Paris and the south of France. His example, deplored by his mother and the country's middle-classes, was followed by the members of the upper classes and by many of the newly enriched industrialists and entrepreneurs of the age.

The great mass of society was slow to change and most people, without the benefits of communications that were to come in later in the century, remained largely ignorant of the way Edward and his set conducted themselves. For most people in Britain, the focal point was the family group and their behaviour was dictated by a fairly rigid set of rules and standards.

FAR LEFT: *A PICNIC IN THE COUNTRYSIDE, 1909*
A vicar and his family enjoy a picnic in the Oxfordshire countryside. The older girl's white blouse, tie and boater, which was the fashionable style for sporting women, suggests that she may have arrived by bicycle from the Oxford Great Western Railway station ☙

LEFT: *THE 'MERRY WIDOW HAT' 1908*
Actress Phyllis le Grand wears a splendid example of a hat that took its name from The Merry Widow, *Franz Lehar's operetta which was the rage in London when it was first performed in 1905* ☙

The father was the indisputable head of the Edwardian household. He was the controller of the family finances, the bread winner and the dispenser of rewards and punishments. Members of the family did not challenge his authority.

Wives played the role of obedient partner, although their personalities defined the parameters of the power they wielded behind the closed front doors of their homes. On the domestic front, household maintenance, meals and looking after the children in their nursery were the prerogatives of the Edwardian wife, while the husband's most domestic task was to look after the wine cellar. The husband also dictated the children's education and family routines like church-going. He set the framework for the family's attitudes towards politics, religion, social relationships and how the family members behaved outside the home.

Most Edwardian families except the very poor kept servants. The households of small wage-earners and artisans might have just a girl living in and a washerwoman coming in once a week.

BELOW: *WEDDING GROUP 1910*
Large hats for the ladies and plenty of flowers are essentials at this well-off family's wedding party which displayed the social status of the family and guests ❦

LEFT: WOMEN ON BOATS, 1900
Women scullers with pretty flowered hats at Kensington on the Thames, speed past a leisurely punt guided by a lady who knows how to wield a pole with grace and decision. The Edwardian middle class woman was not the wilting lily of Queen Victoria's reign and was beginning to challenge male supremacy.

LEFT: *TRYING ON A CORSET, 1900*
Every middle class young woman wanting to display the fasionable Edwardian
hour glass figure needed to wear a corset to achieve it. Putting one on often
required the help of a lady's maid or a helpful husband. In order to make lacing
easier, women hung on to a bar attached to the ceiling which stretched their bodies
while someone laced them up &

The better off would have at least a cook and a general maid, while the upper-middle classes and the wealthy would have several indoor servants and perhaps a gardener and a man in the stables as well.

Servants were provided with accommodation in attics or cellars, and given a uniform. Many servants, sent into service by their own families at an early age, worked for years for the same family and felt a loyalty to them. Often they had a particularly good relationship with the children of the family, being more down-to-earth and approachable than their parents. They would entertain the children with stories of ghosts and witches and other creatures of legend and superstition from their own country workpeople background.

The children's nannies were in a different class from the servants, and came from more educated backgrounds. Their own families were often of the trading classes or were impoverished clergy, but they tended to share the opinions and attitudes of their employers, including their snobbery. Nannies had an unshakeable belief that 'cleanliness was next to godliness'.

Relatives were an important part of the Edwardian family, and felt protected by it. Unmarried aunts, uncles and cousins were an asset in the routines of family life, especially when it came to the care of the children, with whom they often had a special sentimental relationship free from the disciplines that parents felt it essential to insist upon. Unmarried female relatives were a particular blessing to housebound wives because they could exchange gossip with them and discuss intimate matters.

LEFT: *A CORSET ADVERTISEMENT, 1911*
Advertisement for a 'Persephone' corset. Its shape, suggesting the Gibson Girl figure rather than the hour glass, reflected the free, open-air women of the late Edwardian period ❧

RIGHT: *CORSET ADVERTISEMENT, 1912*
Another advertisement for a Persephone corset, its name no doubt intended to conjure up thoughts of the beautiful goddess of spring saved from a life in the gloomy Underworld by Orpheus and his magic lute ❧

Also important to the Edwardian family were the local tradesmen who supplied the household with food and other goods and who often had special relationships with the households they served. Their loyalty, honesty and willingness to serve were highly valued and ensured continuing custom for generations. The trust between customer and supplier was particularly important when orders for goods and taking delivery of them was left to servants.

Another essential member of the Edwardian family was the dog – or dogs: there might be several of them, playing different roles in the domestic scene. Wives might have little pets called Fifi, Dodo or Fluffy, or the pals of the master of the house might be bulldogs, mastiffs, or, in country houses, the pointers, setters, labradors or spaniels suited to a sportsman. Greyhounds and whippets were popular with the poorer classes. For the children, dogs were animated toys that could be taught to obey the orders they would give to servants or employees in adult life. For the servants, dogs were often a nuisance, tearing up carpets and leaving excreta

LEFT: *EARLY VERSION OF A VACUUM CLEANER, 1900*
The vacuum cleaner man with his unwieldy contraption, which would suck up dust and dirt from carpets and other over-upholstered furniture so beloved by well-to-do Victorians ❧

behind pianos and under tables.

Edwardian families were very self-aware, seeing themselves as a social unit, and they called their homes their castle. If they were abroad, working for the greater good of the Empire, they referred to England as Home. Because the home was a symbol for what the family and the nation stood for, it had to look strong. Furniture was solid and dignified and the paintings on the walls reflected a respect for orderly nature under the control of man – a theme repeated in the glass cases full of stuffed birds and showcases filled with seashells and dried seaweed that stood in most drawing rooms.

LEFT: *A GIRL PLAYS AT BEING A MOTHER*
The sailor suit which represented Britain's maritime supremacy was Sunday best for boys and girls alike from the Victorian age up to the 1920s. This well dressed young girl is also the proud possessor of a replica pram which prepared her for her future career in motherhood ❧

FAR LEFT: *EARLY BUS, 1905*
London motor buses introduced in 1905 had solid rubber tyres and every seat on the top deck had a piece of American cloth in case of rain. The top deck was also where men could smoke their cheap, home rolled cigarettes and smelly pipes ❧

RIGHT: *WHAT THE WELL-DRESSED BABY WORE, 1900*
The baby's high pleated bonnet suggests parents inclined to show that they were a social success. Unfortunately, like many of the Edwardian nouveau riche, *they did not understand the word 'chic'* ✥

BELOW: *A NURSE MAID AND HER CHARGE*
Is this a typically severe look of a serious and reliable nursemaid? Or the scowl of a camera shy woman? ✥

LEFT: *THE WINDSORS AND THE ROMANOVS, 1909*
Three generations of two Royal families sit for a portrait during Cowes Week on the Isle of Wight, 1909. From left, the future Edward VIII, Mary, his mother and the future Queen of England; Alexandra, Queen of Great Britain; her granddaughter princess Mary and her daughter Princess Victoria; Czar Nicholas II of Russia, King Edward the VII of Great Britain; Princess Olga of Russia, her mother Empress Alexandra, and her sister Princess Tatiana; the future George V, King of Great Britain; and Princess Marie of Russia. Seated in front are Czarevitch Alexis and Grand Duchess Anastasia, Nicholas and Alexandra's youngest children. The Czar, his wife, and all their children would be executed by the Bolsheviks nine years later ⚜

RIGHT: *ASCOT FASHIONS, 1913*
Two women enjoying the great social event of Ascot, a favourite playground of Edward VII. Unaware of the dark clouds on the European horizon ❧

BELOW: *BOY PULLING CAR WITH HIS TEETH, EARLY 20TH CENTURY*
Feats of strength and daring were much admired in Imperial Britain. Houdini was idolised for his ability to escape from perilous situations and Saxon Brown, 17, for his strength in pulling a one ton motor car by his teeth ❧

BELOW: *AFTERNOON TEA OUTDOORS, 1904*
A typically Edwardian group of the new bourgeoisie with the men in unpretentious working men's caps and the
ladies in fashionable straw boaters ❧

Glorious military and naval events in the history of the Empire, such as the Death of Nelson, Napoleon on Board the Bellerophon, or The Relief of Ladysmith (or Lucknow), as portrayed in large prints, also featured among the wall decorations. Samplers, often the work of the wife or daughters of the house, featured quotations from the Bible or offered sound moral advice: '*If a thing is worth doing it is worth doing well*'.

The Edwardian way of thinking undoubtedly helped to create a self-satisfied society, especially among the middle class. Many poor people tried to emulate them as they struggled out of the swamp of poverty and misery that was still the lot of hundreds of thousands of Britons as the Edwardian era ended, despite the efforts of the Liberal government that had been swept into power in the middle of Edward's reign. But a new perception of what society could be like had begun to stir in the Edwardian age.

ABOVE: *ENJOYING A BEACH OUTING, 1910*
Dogs were a part of all outdoor parties, as long as they behaved themselves like the adults in this sedate group. The tents in the background suggest that the younger members, and the dog, may have gone for a romp in the surf after the photograph was taken ❧

LEFT: *OUTSIDE A TYPICAL MIDDLE-CLASS TERRACE HOUSE, 1905*
Hundreds of thousands of middle-class Edwardians lived in terrace houses like the immortal Mr. Pooter, who lived a conventional life in the suburbs of South London. The man before his garden gate with his son was undoubtedly a Pooter prepared to give up his life for his king and country, which unfortunately many Pooters did ❧

SECTION TWO

The School Years

The rigours of Tom Brown's schooldays were still in evidence until World War 2 in public and grammar schools, especially in those where pupils were boarders. These schools were designed to train middle class youth for the responsibilities of an extended British Empire and instil in them the qualities of loyalty, dedication, fortitude and perseverance. The sucessful product of this form of education was destined to work in far flung corners of the earth in reputable British companies, in the public or military services and commercial or educational organisations which preserved and promoted British interests.

The various means by which students were prepared for life included gamesmanship, a rigid discipline and respect for the pyramid of authority, at the summit of which were God, the King, and the male parent. Most education was lavished on male children, as it was not thought necessary for females to be educated other than in domestic duties and child rearing.

Education was single sex and the

LEFT: *MISS BOWLES' CLASS, 1905*
The girls in this private school were well behaved and allowed a certain freedom of dress and hair style ❦

BELOW: *BOYS' SCHOOL*
Discipline in boys' schools was stricter and some kind of uniform, like wide collars seen here, was obligatory ❦

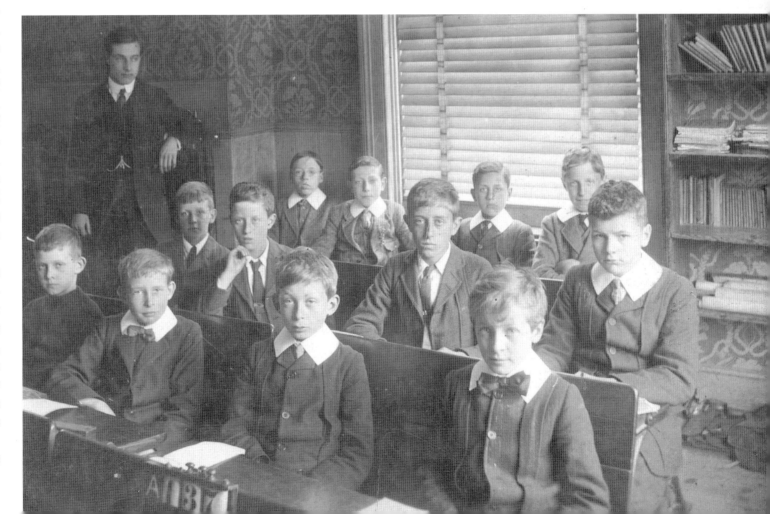

BELOW: *STREET CHILDREN IN HOXTON, 1900*
Hoxton was not a smart residential quarter. The quality of the children's clothes suggest that they may have been second-hand from wealthier families in other parts of London ❧

status of schools related to the various social classes. Eton, Harrow and Winchester, the top educational institutions were the seedbed of the nobility, politics, the higher levels of the Church, and the Law. The new middle-classes and skilled trades had their own establishments and the working classes made do with general education as described by Dickens in Dotheboys Hall.

An effort to improve educational facilities was made in 1902, when responsibility for national education was put in the hands of town and county councils, but secondary education was not organised until 1944 when a Ministry of Education was created.

Private boarding schools were favoured by the middle classes, who believed that they offered a better system of education than both state schools and private day schools. For families with jobs abroad they were the answer to giving their children, especially boys, a grounding in the British way of life. They also had the advantage of relieving the parents of the

LEFT: *START OF SCHOOL HOLIDAYS, 1926*
Students from Ardingly school pile their suitcases onto a wagon at the beginning of the Christmas holidays

tiresome years of adolescence.

Boys at boarding school quickly acquired a team spirit combined with an impulse to break the rules, which, though frowned on and punished, was often overlooked by schoolmasters who admired initiative, as long as it did not disrupt the school system as a whole. Complaints to parents about unruly boys were non-existent and rebellion was dealt with within the school system. This was reassuring to parents, who thus believed that their offspring were enjoying themselves.

The team spirit was fostered by the assumption that your school was the 'best of all schools' and this belief was strengthened by victories on the playing fields. Individuals who helped to achieve

ABOVE: *PREPARATORY CLASS, BRONDESBURY AND KILBURN HIGH SCHOOL, 1910*
Very young students were allowed more informality than the older ones and sat in groups on the floor or round a table

RIGHT: *SCHOOL MILK, 1931*
Free school milk ensured that the children who had not had breakfast received some nourishment during morning lessons

LEFT: *SCHOOL GEOGRAPHY LESSON, 1930 The geography of Britain was not common knowledge to children before the age of railways and road transport, and teachers like this one, invented ingenious ways of holding children's attention* &

victories were awarded with colours in the form of striped blazers, one for each sport, and caps which were worn even in adult life by their proud possesors. To gain such honours boys had to progress through school teams such as juniors, colts, second elevens, fifteens etc. Those who achieved success were immortalised by having their names carved on wooden panels which decorated dining rooms and halls.

Another method of encouraging team spirit was an elaborate system of privileges, many of them created and supported by the boys themselves, in order to preserve the hierarchy and authority of the adolescent community. Systems varied from school to school but there was a consensus on behaviour, which included not allowing new boys to put their hands in trouser pockets or to wear handkerchiefs in breast pockets or tucked into cuffs. Privileges and sanctions changed as the terms went by and promotion by seniority was the norm.

Most boarding schools had an Officers' Training Corps, membership of which was morally obligatory and which, like the real army, instilled in

BELOW: *SCHOOL DINNERS, TOTTENHAM 1944*
Pupils partaking in a wartime school lunch which inevitably included much bread, potatoes and occasionally sausage meat ∽

RIGHT: *SCHOOLBOYS ATTEND A LESSON IN HORTICULTURE, 1932*
Pupils at Clapham Common Springwell House School get a lesson in gardening, hopefully leading them to take up healthy outdoor occupations ∽

ABOVE: BOY COBBLERS, 1942
Useful craftmanship was a part of the school extra-mural activities during the war years. Here a group of boys in Cumberland are learning about cobbling, and will make their own shoes from whatever material is available, including old motor car tyres ❧

BELOW: *SPORTS DAY SPRINT, 1950*
The runners are at the critical stage of a relay race, where a baton pass can mean the difference between triumph and disaster ❧

RIGHT: *SACK RACE ON SPORTS DAY*
Teachers sometimes joined in to cheers or gibes from friendly pupils in 1950, when school relationships had become more informal than in the past ❧

boys a spirit of discipline and encouraged leadership by the awarding of ranks. Drills, manoeuvres and field days gave the system a sense of reality.

At every level of school life boys were subject to a scale of punishments, of which the most severe, but rare, was a caning by the headmaster and the least painful a whacking with a house shoe by the head of the boys' common room. In between was a caning by a prefect, usually voted for by a jury of these arbiters of justice for infractions of house rules.

None of these punishments was traumatic and most were as unavoidable as injuries sustained on the playing field and like these, were often worn as badges of honour by the victims.

Pupils did not receive colours for academic achievements; some were awarded books (not silver cups and medals like the athletes) and supreme distinctions, like success in university entrance examinations, were also marked on honours boards.

Boys of the poorer classes whose fathers were clerks or tradesmen sometimes managed to gain places in the boarding schools by grants awarded for academic achievement but, like boys who attended day school, they were regarded as an inferior class and found it difficult to penetrate the inner circles of boarders.

For parents the boarding school was a status symbol of the same kind as a profession or membership of the right club, even the right tennis club, and continued to be so for many years.

After World War 2 schools were subject to the same changes as society with greater opportunites for all and curricula more adapted to modem life. Education was now a universal right but not sought universally, and few would claim that schooldays were the best days of their lives.

BELOW: *HOUSEWIFERY LESSON*
A washing lesson in the Morden Terrace Housewifery Centre in 1900. This mundane household chore was essential for mothers of large, poor families and girls going into service

LEFT: *FINISHING SCHOOL, 1930*
A group of young ladies compose themselves and read around the fireplace, an activity considered more useful and stimulating than listening to the radio or the gramophone ⌘

RIGHT: *TEACHER RETIRES, 1929*
Mr Popes receives a hearty send-off from his Harrow boys, who wave their traditional boaters in fond farewell ⌘

LEFT: *MRS DEMMICK TEACHING BOYS TO DARN SOCKS, 1940*
This domestic chore, usually considered a female duty, was popularised by publicity given to the Prince of Wales' sock darning skills

SECTION THREE
At The Seaside

By 1900 the seaside holiday had become an essential ingredient of family life in Britain. This form of national recreation, made more accessible by the railways, had turned simple fishing villages into towns by the sea with promenades, piers, wintergardens and terraces of houses with bay windows and views of the waves which Britannia ruled.

The early reputation of seaside resorts as health spas had now faded and the seaside had become a place for hedonist enjoyment, where drinking and flirting were not likely to attract the censorious eyes of home town neighbours. The beaches were a common ground with neat, painted cabins where bathing costumes could be donned with propriety, or picnics enjoyed in comfort. Elsewhere bathers could wriggle into their costumes in tents or behind towels and newspapers. In some resorts there were still bathing cabins which could be dragged out to sea providing total privacy from peeping toms.

A more informal ethos began to emerge after the Great War, when social attitudes began to relax and the advent

LEFT: *DONKEY RIDES*
Donkey rides at Weston-Super-Mare were still a feature of beach entertainment in the 1920s and the nearest that most people would have had to horse riding ≈

BELOW: *VIEW FROM SEASIDE PROMENADE*
Scarborough's early popularity was due not only to the benefits of sea bathing but because it also possessed a mineral spa. The large building in the foreground is the Grand Hotel and the ruin of Scarborough Castle is on the horizon ≈

BELOW: *SANDCASTLE COMPETITION, 1913*
Creating buildings and animal sculptures out of sand was a much admired skill and kept children occupied ☞

of women workers, essential to the war effort, brought about a more companionable relationship between the sexes. Nevertheless, the middle classes still preserved Victorian manners and standards.

The seaside was an ideal place for family holidays, for on the beaches there was an almost classless society, (in some resorts more than others) and children had plenty of space to run about safely. Mothers could sit without the need for a male protector and join in the building of sandcastles, walk alongside their charges on donkey rides and even paddle without embarrassment.

In an age when a pale skin was a mark of those who did not belong to the working classes, mothers of the middle class provided their children with protection against the sun by making them wear large hats, or shelter under parasols.

Those who could afford them paid for deck chairs which not only added to the comfort of sitting on a beach but prevented the sand from seeping into the folds of long skirts.

The formal side of visits to the seaside began to disappear in the 1920s. Thanks to their greater leisure and earning power, people of the industrial areas could now afford the reduced fares offered by railway companies in competition with the new charabanc buses and even tramways, which extended the beach areas of resorts like Blackpool and Southend.

Many of the amenities of the early and prim seaside remained in place for reasons of economy. It was easier to paint rows of bathing cabins or huts than to build new ones and these old and charming cabins continued to play their part as little homes on the beach as well as lovers' arbours at night.

The beach became more a playground and less a terrace for absorbing the

ABOVE: *SEASIDE BONNETS, 1909*
These three little girls keep their complexions fair, a mark of class distinction, with large, lacey broad brimmed bonnets, while looking for shrimps and crabs among the rocks

RIGHT: *BATHING MACHINE, BRIGHTON 1912*
In the evenings bathing machines sometimes served as lovers' 'rendez-vous', according to saucy seaside postcards

health-giving ozone. Adults as well as children played cricket and football or flew kites in the wide open spaces, supervised by attendants who ensured that these activities were enjoyed without inconvenience to others.

The pier was a centre for varied attractions for all classes and ages. There were penny slot machines, that revealed the goings on in a haunted house or offered a peep through a keyhole to see what the butler saw (which was always disappointing). There was a theatre where performances of magic or minstrel shows entertained everyone and there were seats for fishermen hoping to catch plaice or flounders. For young men and women the pier was primarily a promenade where an examination could be made before the striking up of an acquaintanceship. Some of the goings on of the period were recorded on 'saucy' cartoon picture postcards which have become collectors' items. The beach as a place of entertainment also developed technical innovations such as pier trains, trains that skirted the beach, as at Brighton, and chutes for entering

BELOW: *LEAPFROG ON BEACH, 1930*
The East Kent resorts were the first to be patronised by London office workers, who, before the railways, arrived by sailing wherries down the Thames ⚘

ABOVE: *FEMALE BATHERS, 1910*
Though the style of bathing costumes was demure, the woven cotton fabric revealed more than was intended when wet ❦

ABOVE: *BY THE SEA, 1920s*

LEFT: *MARGATE BEACH, 1920s*
A family enjoys a day out on Margate beach ❦

LEFT: *THE WATER CHUTE, BOURNEMOUTH 1927*
Chutes, beach ball courts, swings and roundabouts brought bathing suited men and women into a physical intimacy unknown before World War I ❧

NOTICE

NO RESPONSIBILITY IS UNDERTAKEN BY THE CORPORATION IN RESPECT OF ANY MISHAP WHICH MAY OCCUR TO ANY PERSON USING THIS WATER CHUTE.

LEFT: *FAMILY PORTRAIT ON BEACH, 1900*
For children, the joyful freedom to lark about was tempered by family photographs,
essential in the early days of box cameras ❧

ABOVE: *SEASIDE PADDLE, 1950*
Exploration of the strange and mysterious world of rock pools and seaweeds was both
exciting and unintentionally educational ❧

the water with a splash. There were also spaces, sometimes on the piers themselves, reserved for fairgrounds with scenic railways, helter skelters, merry-go-rounds, a Ferris wheel and other attractions which became ever more thrilling and expensive.

Many of the old, simple pleasures continued, however, and provided whole families with the excitement and joy of catching crabs, netting prawns and shrimps and collecting shells, not to mention the incomparable pleasure of teaching young ones to swim, with water wings if necessary, and recording the event with a box Brownie camera.

In the thirties, the social changes wrought by women's emancipation, the jazz age, and popular newspapers were reflected in life at the seaside, which had always encouraged a sense of freedom and anonymity from the ties of home. This became apparent in the style of swimwear of both men and women, which became briefer and more revealing, and in the growing popularity of 'palais de danse' where greater physical contact was encouraged by dances like the foxtrot and tango.

BELOW: *PERFORMANCE ON SCARBOROUGH BEACH, 1907*
Clowns were later replaced by more sophisticated entertainment by minstrels and music hall performers in proper pier theatres ❧

ABOVE: *SHRIMPING, HUNSTANTON 1905*
The nets were pushed under fronds of seaweed to capture the shrimps and crabs sheltering in the cool darkness at low tide ❧

RIGHT: *BATHING BEAUTIES OF 1936*
Three happy young women sampling the joys of the seaside, on a mat at the bottom of a slide or Helter Skelter ❧

LEFT: *KEEPING FIT BY BRIGHTON'S PALACE PIER, 1935*
The mania for keeping fit spread from Germany through images of bronzed, muscular 'Hitler Youth' and was copied in Britain by the Health and Beauty movement

The advent of holidays abroad, after World War 2, brought a temporary decline to the popularity of the British seaside. Holidays in Spain for £25 were as affordable as holidays at home. The average earning power of the public made two holidays a year possible, however, and the British holiday returned to favour both for its traditional delights and its encouragement of carnivals, competitions, and party spirit.

World War One

LEFT: *AIR RAID SHELTER ON THE STRAND, 1918*
The fear of bomb dropping German Zeppelins led to the building of air raid shelters protected by sandbags, in this case set up by the YMCA ⁊

BELOW: *SOLDIER AND HIS WIFE, 1918*
The fearsome prospect of separation and death created a need for the reassurance of a photographic record ⁊

In September 1914, nobody believed that a war beween the Allied powers and the Central powers could last long; in Britain most people thought that it would be over by Christmas. They were tragically mistaken, for after an initial victory at the Battle of the Marne which prevented the occupation of Paris, the combating armies settled down into a war of attrition from trenches which were mud ditches in winter and embankments of clay and sand bags in the summer.

By 1916 the numbers of dead were mounting and war work at home was increasing. Every effort was made to outdo the German armament factories and to boost the food supply, which had decreased owing to German submarine warfare. A major effort was required in order to bring about a decisive victory and the battle of the Somme was launched in support of the French armies at Verdun. The result on the first day was 60,000 casualties, which included 20,000 dead. The supply of medical equipment and supplies was inadequate to deal with such large numbers.

The disaster of the Somme was one of several errors in statesmanship and military leadership, among them the failure at Gallipolli to neutralise the Ottoman Empire support for Germany, the death of 245,000 men at Ypres near the village of Passchendaele, and the inconclusive battle of Jutland. Here, more British ships than German were sunk but further German naval action was prevented. By 1918 the German army was back on the Marne but the American allies, who had arrived in 1917, became a decisive factor in bringing about Germany's defeat, though not ambitions. Many soldiers, including one, Adolf Hitler, continued to believe that victory had been snatched unfairly from imminent success.

The intimations of the seriousness of the war were first brought home to the public by the growing number of men in uniform, often seen at railway stations as they left for the front or arriving, wounded in muddy and bloody uniforms, at Waterloo and Victoria stations.

LEFT: *SOUP KITCHEN 1917*
Following the worst year of the war, food was running out owing to U-boat attacks. In order to alleviate the life of the homeless many organisations like the Salvation Army provided free food ⚜

The shelling of Hartlepool by German warships and the bombings by enemy Zeppelins, and Gotha bomber aircraft with its 1000 lb bombs, brought the war home, increasing the hatred of all things German. Anyone with a German name became a target, and even Alsatian dogs were ill-treated in the streets. The British royal family name of 'Saxe Coburg Gotha' was changed to Windsor, though in some towns and villages it was accepted that German names often belonged to loyal British families.

The rationing of food, which was under threat from the German U-boat campaign in the Atlantic, also aroused civilian fears and sometimes selfishness as people queued for meagre rations to supplement a daily menu of tea, bread and dripping, potatoes and other root crops and scraps of meat.

ABOVE: *MAN SELLS WAR BONDS, 1915*
The increasing need and cost of the production of armaments was financed by war bonds promoted both in Britain and the USA by celebrities like Douglas Faibanks and Mary Pickford ☙

RIGHT: *BRITISH FLYING ACE, ALBERT BALL*
This aeroplane, a single engined biplane was Britain's answer to the German fighter aircraft and air aces like Albert Hall, to Baron Richthoven, the Red Baron, 1914-18 ☙

LEFT: *READING POSTER 1917*
This mother and her children are reading a poster which offers the public protection in a cellar from air attacks ❧

RIGHT: *CHRISTMAS SHOPPING DURING THE GREAT WAR*
The Christmas lull which troops had observed in the first year of the war had given way to unrelenting fighting. Soldiers coming home on Christmas leave in 1917 found it difficult to adapt to domestic celebrations ❧

The effect of the war on family life was not, at first, dramatic but conscription increased the numbers involved in the war. The young men joined up and those that did not have the misfortune to become front line combatants enjoyed their new freedom, as did the women released from their domestic duties who joined the VAD (Voluntary Aid Detachments). Their work became increasingly essential in hospitals for the wounded but caused traumatic shock to young girls, who had never seen anything worse than a cut finger.

Leisure time at home was spent in knitting scarves, gloves and socks for soldiers, or making up parcels with food and tobacco. Church going became more regular, especially for those whose sons were at the front-line and who lived in dread of communications from the War Office. Many mantelpieces had a photograph of an officer, though there were fewer in the homes of the poor whose sons were Tommies in the 'poor bloody infantry'.

The war brought to the British people an awareness of vulnerability which was

LEFT: *PARCELS OF BOOKS ARE SENT TO SOLDIERS*
Parcels were prepared by civilians to send to wounded soldiers in hospitals in France and Britain ❧

RIGHT: *BARRAGE BALLOONS OVER LONDON*
These forced attackers to keep high and made bombing difficult, but meant that bombs fell indiscriminately on homes as well as military targets ❧

FAR RIGHT: *SOLDIER AT HOME ON LEAVE, 1915*
Luckily, this soldier managed to get leave at Christmas so could spend it with his family ❧

difficult to believe after so many years of Pax Britannica. In the reigns of Victoria and Edward, and growing public awareness there came disillusionment with military and political leaders. It also brought a new respect for women who had kept 'the homefires burning' (in the words of the song writer Ivor Novello) and for the working class men, who had been prepared to give up their lives for their country and deserved 'a home fit for heroes to live in'.

The morale of the nation was not at risk, but political leaders and the media combined to keep up everyone's spirits once the numbers of casualties began to be known. The religious faith of the past gave everyone strength and inspired legends of angels that appeared at crucial battles and the Virgin Mary comforting the wounded.

Items of food and household items like mugs and plates carried pictures of military leaders and housewives were applauded for their contribution to the war effort. For those who were homeless or lacked home care, soup kitchens were set up and were besieged by adults and children. Over a million women had joined in the war effort and they were praised for skills which no one had thought them capable of. Even children were encouraged to identify with Britain as in verses such as

This is the house that Jack built
This is the bomb that hit the house that Jack built
This is the Hun that made the bomb that hit the house that Jack built
And this is the gun to kill the Hun that made the bomb
That hit the house that Jack built.

The most potent weapons in the propaganda war were film, invented just before the war and its leading actor, an Englishman called Charlie Chaplin. From Hollywood Chaplin spread the idea of a little man who could survive any crisis and smile at it. This spirit echoed the feelings of the nation and when the film *Shoulder Arms* appeared in 1918 it was an instant and universal success.

For families, the end of the war was a welcome relief and every street in every

BELOW: *HOMES DESTROYED BY ZEPPELINS, 1915*
Raids on London left homes wrecked and their inhabitants wounded or dead, but did not destroy the morale of the people ❧

LEFT: *BY LAMPLIGHT, 1915*
British soldiers gathered round
paraffin lamps to amuse each other
with stories and anecdotes. Self made
entertainment included songs and
ribald jokes about the enemy ⚔

BELOW: TROOPS MARCH TO
TRENCHES AT YPRES
British troops, seen in silhouette as
they march towards the trenches
where 245,000 lives were lost in this
unsuccessful attempt to gain a few
metres of ground ⚔

BELOW: *FIRST AID DRILL*
Children staged Red Cross first aid drills, but before the war was over, many of these young girls would be facing the reality of caring for badly wounded soldiers ❧

town in Britain celebrated the victory, before returning to a normal life. However, resemblance to the life of the Edwardians would gradually disappear.

Though there was little damage at home the post-war effect was profound, creating a distrust of national leaders and a public that looked with favour on the revolution that had occurred in Russia in 1917. People showed antipathy to war and there was wide public acclaim for films like *All Quiet on the Western Front* and books like *Cry Havoc* by the popular journalist, Beverly Nichols.

The majority of Britons however, remained undismayed and there was an increase in the spirit of helpfulness towards others. Notable exceptions included those who took advantage of the circumstances to indulge in crime and vandalism, including a band of thugs called the Napoos, who attacked women with longhair by cutting off their plaits in broad daylight.

SECTION FIVE
Between The Wars

The end of World War I brought many families together, as they rejoiced at the return of peaceful life or mourned the loss of loved ones. The civilian population had escaped almost unscathed and soon returned to pre-war habits of family gatherings and holidays, but there was a growing desire among the young for independence and freedom from the ties of home.

The young wanted to lead their own lives, but many did not have the earning power to be able to do so. The home remained, therefore, the base in which the new spirit of youth and enterprise struggled to establish itself and there was a certain amount of shared family pastimes. One of these was the gramophone, which later became a piece of furniture known as the radiogram. The gramophone had started off as a rotating cylinder on which the vibrations of sounds were engraved and reproduced when a needle with a diaphragm passed over it. The cylinder later became a flat disc and was available in a box with a speaker attached to the needle carriage. This portable gramophone soon became both an essential part of the household and a portable instrument which could be taken on outings to youth parties at the seaside, where dancing in bathing suits fostered a new sensual intimacy.

Music enabled young people to express feelings that had hitherto remained hidden or silent, in eras when it was customary not to 'wear your heart on your

LEFT: *SAXOPHONE SECTION*
The Henry Hall orchestra ended the daily BBC broadcasts in 1937 with the theme song Here's to the next time, *a melody which was followed by the national anthem at 11pm punctually* ⅋

RIGHT: *LISTENING TO THE RADIO, 1920s*
The earliest form of popular radio reception was by means of a crystal sensitive to sound waves on which a wire relayed sound to earphones. This was followed by the radio valve which fulfilled the same purpose more accurately ⅋

BELOW: *DANCE BAND REHEARSING, 1927*
Savoy Hill saw the birth of broadcasting and the Savoy Hotel was the home of London's distinguished dance orchestras. Here the Percival Mackay Dance Band performs with Monte Ryan, the cabaret artiste ❧

BELOW: *SUBURBAN SEMI IN THE 1930's*
Most suburban houses emulated the country homes of the well off with gables, bay windows, exposed beams and porticoes over the front door ☞

sleeve'. The new freedom of expression gave rise to two of the world's greatest songwriters. Irving Berlin, already known through songs like *A Pretty Girl is Like a Melody*, now became more famous through film musicals such as those starring the world's most popular dancers, Ginger Rogers and Fred Astaire. Berlin was a simple man with limited musical education but his fellow composer of the period was a sophisticated socialite, Cole Porter. Porter's melodies and lyrics gave expression to an era when the world was recovering from the years of the Depression, and optimism reigned in tunes like *Anything Goes* and *I Get a Kick Out of You*.

Another shared interest in families was the radio or wireless, which relayed news, drama and sports events through a British Broadcasting Company. (subsequently the BBC) in 1922. Wireless telegraphy, invented by an Italian, Gugliemo Marconi, brought a new dimension to twentieth century life, rendering the outside world a part of home life and a sounding board for the different opinions of members of a family

A form of outside entertainment which also shaped family life was the cinema or picture house, which from simple beginnings in shed-like buildings became palatial and exotic, with architecture in Egyptian, Mexican and Arab styles. The cinema, at first with silent comedy films which all ages in a family could enjoy, gradually turned to romantic dramas and historical epics, provoking discussion and sometimes controversy, to musicals, which lifted the spirits after the dull years following the financial crisis of 1929-32.

The divergences of opinions in families after the Great War soon began to widen and produced conflicting views on friends, fashion, social manners, literature and entertainment. Very few parents could approve of the more critical view of life of Noel Coward's *Vortex*, T.S. Eliot's *The Hollow Men*, D.H. Lawrence's *Lady Chatterley's Lover*, or Evelyn Waugh's *Decline and Fall*, which appeared to them destructive and iconoclastic. Music, too, was a subject of controversy: the jazz of black musicians like Louis Armstrong, and bands with undignified names such as 'Miff Mole and his Harlem Footwarmers' were difficult to accept, and the so-called classical music of Gershwin or Ravel was offensive. The new medium of cinema was also a bone of contention with films like Marlene Dietrich's *The Blue Angel* and Boris Karloff's *Frankenstein* suggesting dangerous values and ideas. Sometimes public reaction was considered violent: Jewish sculptor Jacob Epstein's *Rima,* placed in Hyde Park, was daubed with creosote and his *Adam*, with its large penis, was attacked by a woman with an umbrella.

However, everyone was proud of national achievements, such as those of Amy Johnson and her husband Jim Mollison who undertook intrepid, long distance flights to S. Africa and the Atlantic, and Jean Batten, who flew to Australia. Speed alone became a reason for admiration and when Lieutenant Stainforth broke the air speed record at 407 miles per hour and Malcolm Campbell the land speed record at 253 miles per hour, the nation rejoiced.

The hopes and aspirations of the post war ere were doomed, however. The depression years following the Wall Street Crash of 1929, though not felt immediately in Europe, made jobs difficult to find and industrial employment was at a low ebb, as coal mines and factories closed and men were obliged to seek government financial assistance, then known as the Dole.

In the poorer regions visits to the pawnshop became habitual with wives hocking their husbands' clothes or family possessions and redeeming them at the end of the week on payday. Sometimes these remained uncollected and ended up being sold cheaply to others.

As the decade leading to World War 2 unfolded, conditions in Britain improved. Nevertheless, the industral workers of the north joined together in hunger marches to focus attention on their desperation, and there were other problems looming. Some, concerned by the apparent inactivity of government, supported the new political party of Oswald Moseley, who proposed a government like that of Mussolini in Italy. Numerous women, including housewives of

LEFT: *POLICE OFFICER CHASES SKINNY DIPPERS, HYDE PARK, 1925*
One of the new type of female constables who pioneered the employment of women in the forces of law and order ❦

FAR LEFT: WOMAN USING A POLICE CALL BOX
Though street crime was not common in the 1930s the police provided special phone boxes for emergency use ❦

LEFT: *CINEMA SHOWS 'ENEMIES OF WOMEN'*
Crowds outside the St James's Picture Theatre in the Strand, London, wait to see a new movie by Clara Bow, the 'It' girl who personified female glamour in 1923

ABOVE: CITY OF WESTMINSTER
St Mary-le-Strand in London's popular theatreland of the 1930s

FAR RIGHT: *EDWARD VIII ABDICATES TO MARRY MRS SIMPSON*
The abdication of Edward VIII in 1936 shocked and split the nation, though George VI and his wife Elizabeth soon won everyone's hearts

all classes, followed his leadership and joined mass keep fit and beauty classes in Hyde Park. The opposition to Moseley came from the Communist party, incensed at the lack of support for republican Spain, which was about to succumb to fascist forces under General Franco.

The nation was divided and the situation was aggravated by the abdication of the popular King Edward VIII to marry a twice divorced American, Wallis Simpson. These divisions would not heal until its future was threatened by a former admirer of Britain, Adolf Hitler.

One saving grace of this era of mixed cultures and ideas was popular music. The musical was the opera of the people and created imaginary worlds in which romance and gaiety won through. Even after the war, the illusion was sustained by musicals such as 'South Pacific' by Rogers and Hammerstein.

The Star

THE LONDONER'S EVENING PAPER

No. 15,139.   ONE PENNY.   THURSDAY, DECEMBER 10, 1936.   RADIO : Page Ten.   WEATHER : Page Three.

THE SPEAKER IN COMMONS ANNOUNCES

ABDICATION

THE DUKE OF YORK TH' NEW KING

KING EDWARD'S MESSAGE:—"I RENOU THE THRONE FOR MYSELF AN FOR MY DESCENDANTS"

FINAL AND IRREVOCAB

RENUNCIATION DOCUMENT WITN BY HIS THREE BROTHERS

KING EDWARD VIII

THE KING'S MESSAGE TO PARLIAMENT, ANNOUNCING HIS WAS READ BY THE SPEAKER (CAPT. FITZROY) IN HOUSE OF COMMONS THIS AFTERNOON.
THE SPEAKER ALSO ANNOUNCED THE ACCESSION T OF THE DUKE OF YORK.

The message had been handed to the Speaker by Mr. Baldw

After long and anxious consideration I have determined to renounce the throne, to which I succeeded on the death of my father, and I am now communicating this my final and irrevocable decision.

Realising, as I do, the gravity of this step I can only hope that I shall have the understanding of my peoples in the decision I have taken, and the reasons

the stability of the and the happiness of

I. EDWARD GREAT BRITAIN THE BRITISH D THE SEAS, KI INDIA DO HER IRREVOCABLE DETERMI TO RENOUNCE THE THRONE FOR

LEFT: *UNEMPLOYED PEOPLE*
Unemployed people, victims of the Depression, aroused much sympathy as well as anger, which lead to the Hunger Marches of 1932 ❧

RIGHT: *GRETA GARBO, 1931*
Despite the Depression, or perhaps as morale builders, film companies made films starring glamorous people like Greta Garbo ❧

FAR RIGHT: *FRED ASTAIRE AND GINGER ROGERS*
Fred Astaire and Ginger Rogers made their film Flying Down to Rio *in 1933 and their vitality and gaiety of spirit echoed the improving situation of the economy* ❧

RIGHT: *GETTING WATER*
Thirsty children in London parks drank water from drinking water pumps in the 1930s when there was no money for bottled mineral drinks ❧

SECTION SIX

World War Two

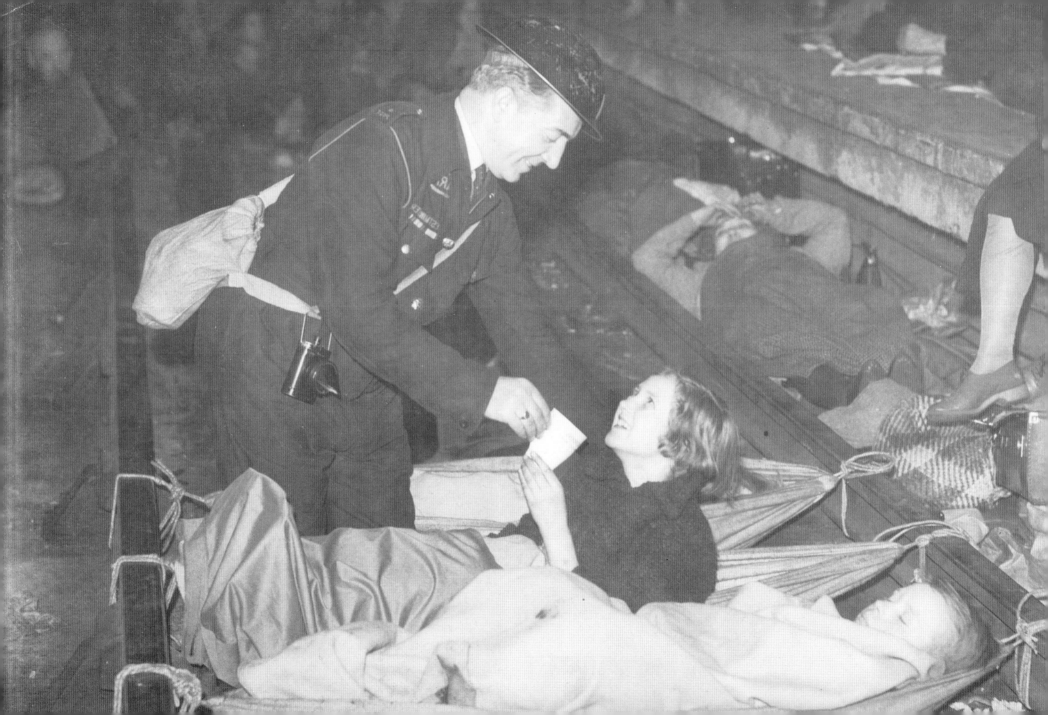

When war broke out in September 1939, there was none of the patriotic fervour of 1914. The British people of all classes were dismayed, having been buoyed up by Neville Chamberlain's announcement that there would be 'Peace in our time' after his meeting with Hitler in 1936.

At first, as no attacks were forthcoming it seemed there might still be a compromise, but after the disaster of Dunkirk such hopes were crushed and the queues at enlistment centres lengthened. Fathers set about digging air raid shelters in their gardens, or serving as air raid wardens or the Home Guard, while wives worked in the auxiliary services. Few believed that the war could be contained in Europe as in 1914, but Churchill's famous words

'We will fight on the beaches, we will fight in the towns, we will never give in.'

inspired families throughout the land.

It was necessary of course that everyone should collaborate in defeating the enemy and one of the essential means for doing so was by keeping morale high. A way of life had to be maintained and the most important ingredient was the provision of adequate food supplies. This was the responsibility of the Ministry of Food, which announced that the government had a plan which would keep everyone fighting fit while releasing ships and men in the merchant marine for combat duties. The plan was to ration food and this was immediately put into force by the issuing of ration books for essential items.

Families pored over the instructions and complained, as families do, but everyone agreed on the necessity of conserving food supplies. The mothers and housewives bore the brunt of the new gastronomy and with the help of the Ministry of Food Advice Bureau, set about producing palatable and satisfying meals from 3.5 ozs of meat, (sausages were not included but difficult to obtain) 2 ozs of butter, between 2 and 8 ozs of cheese, 1 egg and a packet of dried eggs (received every four weeks) and other small amounts of ingredients such as cooking fats, sugar, and milk. Ingenious and capable housewives bottled or dried seasonal fruits and vegetables.

LEFT: *SHELTERING AT ALDWYCH DURING THE BLITZ, 1940*
Aldwych tube station was an important air raid shelter and the crowds that slept on the tube platforms at night were the subject of an important series of drawings by the sculptor Henry Moore

BELOW: *TEA IN UNDERGROUND SHELTER*
During air attacks the people in underground air raid shelters were comforted with cups of tea served by willing volunteers who made gallons of 'the cup that cheers'

Woman power became essential to keep things going, at first on a volunteer basis but then, in 1942, by conscription. Not everyone agreed on women becoming involved in certain activities and some still believed that a woman's place was in the home. Of the six million women who had won the right to work since the Great War, two million were still in domestic service and the rest in low paid jobs in commerce and factories. It was hardly surprising that many of them rushed to volunteer in women's services such as the ATS (Auxiliary Territorial Service), the WAAF (Women's Auxiliary Air Force), the WVS (Women's Voluntary Service – who were unpaid) and the WLA (Womens Land Army) and other service organisations.

It was not long before it was realised that women were as capable as men at skilled industrial work, such as ferrying aircraft from factories to RAF airfields, and manning anti-aircraft batteries. They even had their own Women's Searchlight Regiment which pinpointed enemy invaders and beamed in crippled allied aircraft.

BELOW: *TAKING COVER*
Children taking shelter during air raids often thought of it as an adventure and shared the indomitable spirit of the adults

ABOVE: *EVACUEES ON CORNER*
Evacuee children were grouped together to be taken away from the danger zones. Those in this picture have not gathered together their belongings as they may have already been loaded on a coach ❧

LEFT: *MATRON AND EVACUEES*
Young evacuee children had to learn to look after themselves, carrying their own suitcases and adapting to living in strange homes in different parts of the country ❧

LEFT: *SURVIVORS WALKING THROUGH BOMBED STREETS, 1942*
After a raid on Canterbury the survivors carried on their lives in their ruined town, thankful that the cathedral had been spared ☙

Women were paid less than men and often ran a home as well as their war job. By their efforts and courage women were established as equal to men, changing the face of British society. Their courage in the face of adversity was especially evident during the years of the Blitz, when German incendiary and explosive bombs destroyed the centres of many cities and deaths occurred in thousands and numbers of wounded reached tens of thousands. During this critical period, women ran first aid posts, organised the evacuation of children, drove lorries loaded with food to affected areas, found homes for the bombed out, and sorted clothes for those who had literally lost everything. The unity of the nation was assured by the public spirit and everyone joined,

RIGHT: *RATIONS AND RATION BOOK*
The ration book was an essential household document and allowed 4 rashers of bacon, one real egg and some ounces of powdered ones, a few ounces of sugar cooking fat and vegetables per person, per week ⌘

LEFT: *DELIVERY FOR WATLING STREET, 1941*
The postman standing among the rubble in a London street had an almost impossible task but his job was a part of the morale-building determination to keep life as normal as possible ❧

RIGHT: *MILKMAN MAKING DELIVERIES, 1941*
Milk deliveries were important for those who found it difficult to get to shops but they continued as long as posible ❧

FAR RIGHT: *WATCHING FROM THE DOORWAY*
British children emerging from a shelter after an air raid were curious to see what damage had been done ❧

in one form or another, to carry on as normal a life as possible. Children went to schools, though many were sent abroad for safety. Seaside holidays continued, though many beaches were out of bounds and full of barbed wire and mines. Cinemas, along with air raid shelters, were well patronised and showed stirring and inspiring films such as: *Citizen Kane, The Wizard of Oz, Gone with the Wind, In Which We serve* and *Casablanca*, to name just a few. Artists were enrolled to record the war effort including Henry Moore, who drew the crowds in underground shelters, Paul Nash who painted the skies of the air Battle of Britain and Richard Eurich, of seascapes of the south coast. The spirit of the people became vocal with a popular song *We'll Hang Up Our Washing On The Siegfried Line* and the haunting melody of *White Christmas* by an American, Irving Berlin.

Radio played the most important part of all in national comunication because it was accessible to all, and informed everyone of the state of the conflict. The voices of the news presenters were

BELOW: *MOTHERS AND THEIR BABIES, 1941*
Evacuee mothers with their babies, often left homeless by the bombs and with husbands away, were cared for by official and voluntary organisations which supplied blankets, food and shelter

BELOW: *CHILDREN IN GAS MASKS, 1941* *Children taking part in a gas mask drill at an LCC residential school near Windsor. They often thought it was all a bit of a lark and, like most children, were protected as much as possible from the real horrors of war*

LEFT: *HOMELESS FAMILY*
Until it happened it was difficult to accept the idea of being left homeless, with all one's posessions gone. This family from Liverpool was waiting for help from one of the various bodies which looked after victims and rehoused in a safe country town ⚭

RIGHT: *WOMAN KISSES
RETURNING SOLDIER,
1940*
*The woman leaning over a
barrier is evidently overjoyed
at his return, a scene very
different from those at
departure stations* ☙

LEFT: *ANOTHER HOMELESS FAMILY, 1941*
This family from Portsmouth, after a raid on their city, have an uncertain immediate future but in their temporary van home manage to survive on sandwiches and cups of tea ❧

LEFT: *WW II CHILDREN, 1941*
Bomb victims tried to salvage what they could from the wreckage of their homes. These two children have rescued a makeshift bed, and some kind carer has supplied bread and jam as a temporary panacea ⅋

RIGHT: *BLITZ ON WESTMINSTER*
The survival of some familiar landmark raised the people's spirits and hopes for improved conditions. Big Ben, like St Paul's, hardened people's resolve and determination to survive and win ⅋

BELOW: *EVACUEES ON TRAIN*
Evacuees looking out of a train window on their way to a temporary safe home in the country or abroad, look justifiably nervous

made known in order to vouchshafe the authenticity of broadcasts and prevent confusion with Lord Haw Haw's broadcasts from Hamburg. Entertainers like Tommy Handley of ITMA, who kept up the spirits of those in service as well as civilians, and Vera Lynne, who came to be known as the Forces' Sweetheart, became beacons of hope and optimism, as in the most popular of sentimental ballads *A Nightingale Sang In Berkeley Square.* Curiously enough this was rivalled by a German song called *Lilli Marlene.* By 1942 Britain and her allies were beginning to feel that a long term struggle might prove victorious and when General Montgomery drove the Germans back at El Alamein on the borders of Egypt 'the end of the beginning' as Churchill told the nation, was in sight.

By 1945 the European war was over and Britain was embarking in another new and vibrant era of its history.

Post War Britain

PENSIONS and ALLOWANCES
CHANGE IN OFFICE OF PAYMENT

In the years between the end of the war and 1950 the main task for most families was the re-establishment of a home. War-time duties of various kinds, either in the services abroad or in the support of organisations or factories in Britain had made family life either impossible or at least extremely difficult. Those whose homes had been destroyed or damaged had to seek new ones, perhaps in places like Stevenage or Harlow where the government was setting up new towns, or to repair or refurbish those not too badly damaged. Gardens where Anderson air raid shelters had been installed had to be returned to their natural state.

Household goods had to be replaced, often with items made from the plastics which had been developed by wartime industry. Wardrobes of dull, well-worn clothes could be replaced by new fashions, especially Christian Dior's romantic 'New Look' of 1947, which used yards of fabric. Not everyone could afford originals, of course, and it took a lot of saving of ration coupons to buy enough material to make copies at home. Ingenious women would use parachute silk and other material found in war surplus stores, and men found naval duffle coats and airmen's leather jackets useful and hard-wearing.

More serious for many families were the problems of psychological adjustment between men and women who had been separated for months or years in different

LEFT: *FAMILY LIVING IN LEAKY HUT*
The war had left many homes damaged or destroyed and a programme of rebuilding and repairs was set up. Here George Wallace MP is listening to a mother living in a leaky hut with three young children ❧

FAR LEFT: *FAMILY ALLOWANCE DAY*
The Stratford mother in this photo is picking up her first family allowance in August 1946. Five shillings a week per child was not a fortune but it was evidence of government concern for the welfare of ordinary people ❧

LEFT: *FAMILY BICYCLE*
After the war, in 1948, it was a joy to get out of towns and enjoy the countryside with the whole family ⌘

RIGHT: *PEOPLE ATTEND MOBILE CLINIC, 1946*
Concern for the nation's health aroused by the war created public services like this one, to provide diptheria vaccines for babies from mobile vans ॐ

circumstances and between parents and their children who had grown into strangers, without parental guidance and the loving intimacy of family life.

There were many broader aspects of post-war life and the future to be considered, too, such as peacetime jobs, domestic duties, and children's education. The more conservative view was that Britain was a country with a world-wide empire and a successful industrial and commercial base and would regain its pre-war position by dedication and enterprise. This was not the view of a majority of the population, especially the working- class part of it that had been in the front line of the war during the Blitz and the youth of the country, who had inherited the restless spirit of the 1930s. Neither group had much faith in the promises of the politicians who had been in authority during the two world wars and the economic depression that had marked much of the first half of the century.

Working-class Britons looked for an improvement in their standards of living and the young wanted opportunities and freedom from the social restraints imposed by a class-ridden society so that work success could be decided by merit and initiative. The writer J. B. Priestley, author of the popular novel The Good Companions, had sounded the trumpet note of the post-war period when he said in a radio broadcast that there was no use in looking back to a pre-war world, and that the future lay in community and creativity.

This new spirit led to the feeling, especially among the young, that it was necessary to get rid of 'yesterday's men' and bring in those who would implement the proposals of the widely approved Beveridge Plan. This, proposed in 1942 during the darkest days of the war, aimed at the elimination of unemployment and a

BELOW: *GIRLS LISTEN TO PHONOGRAPH*
These two little girls may have been fans of Bing Crosby, the crooner who became a popular idol

LEFT: *ELVIS*
Elvis Presley with his hip gyrating antics expressed the rebellious spirit of the post war generation of the 1950s and songs like Jailhouse Rock *became anthems of youth* ✄

general improvement in working conditions allied to the creation of a social security system. This strong desire for a change of direction led to the rejection of the wartime hero and national idol Winston Churchill and his Conservative Party at the general election of 1945. Clement Attlee and the Labour Party were now in power with a strong socialist programme to be implemented.

The new Labour government's nationalisation programme was quickly put into effect and within three years the coal industry, the railways and road haulage, civil aviation, the gas and electricity industries and the Bank of England had all been nationalised. While all these things brought about changes in family life relative to

LEFT: *LONDON'S FIRST SELF-SERVICE STORE*
Mrs Archer and her five year-old daughter are selecting a basket in a supermarket at Wood Green, North London and looking excited at the prospect of their visit to the endless shelves of provisions available in 1948 ❦

LEFT: *FAMILY RELOCATES TO PREFAB, 1946*
Many families whose homes were damaged or destroyed during the war moved into temporary mobile homes like Mr and Mrs Stewart ૐ

RIGHT: *WATCHING TELEVISION*
By 1950 television had become an essential piece of household furniture and families spent evenings together watching news events or serilaised dramas known familiarly as 'soap operas' ૐ

RIGHT: *GYPSY HORSE FAIR, 1950*
Before the war gypsies were largely
Romanies with their own culture.
Though maintaining their nomadic way
of life, after the war they began to
integrate in the commercial life of the
country, running horse fairs and funfairs
and providing services as tinkers and
scrap iron traders ⤶

individual family circumstances, the
beginnings of what soon came to be
called the Welfare State at this time
affected all families. Family allowances,
better old age pensions and the
formation of the National Health
Service were welcomed by everyone.
There was a consensus of opinion that
these improved conditions of life were
opening up new opportunities and
offering a life-style freedom that the
young embraced eagerly.

For the young, the post-war years
were more than a time of opportunity,
they were a breeding ground of a new
youth culture and, like most cultures,
required a theme and an anthem.

BELOW: *BRITISH GI BRIDE WITH HER DAUGHTER*
Fraternisation between US troops and British females led to
romantic attachments, many of them permanent. Here Mrs
Bruce Lawrence is seen leaving Waterloo station with her six-
month old daughter to join her husband in America ❧

RIGHT: *INTERIOR OF A HOUSEBOAT*
At a time when housing was scarce some people chose to live
on houseboats on the River Thames and continued to do so,
like this family who thus avoided expensive ground rents ❧

ROYAL ALBERT HALL

(MANAGER: C.S.TAYLOR)

HALL

MENADE
AL
N LONDON

1ST AT 7.30.

CIS
EL

OPIN
ZT

The B.B.C. Presents   53rd Season

HENRY WOOD

PROMENADE CONCERTS

The B.B.C
NY ORCHESTRA

The LONDON
IONIC ORCHESTRA

The LONDON
NY ORCHESTRA

JULY 19 – SEPT 13

AT 7·30 PM

SUNDAYS EXCEPTED

Conductors:
**SIR ADRIAN BOULT
BASIL CAMERON
SIR MALCOLM SARGENT**
Associate Conductor
STANFORD ROBINSON

LEFT: *POSTER FOR THE PROMS, 1947*
Fans of the Promenade Concerts which were started by Henry Wood and made classical music available to everyone ⤚

RIGHT: *SALVATION ARMY WOMEN SINGING IN STREET*
The Salvation Army, a world wide movement started by William Booth which combines religion with welfare and has saved innumerable people from poverty and distress ⤚

As models for their new society the young looked across the Atlantic to America, the birthplace of the jazz age where the swing music of bands like that of war-time favourite Glen Miller was giving way to the hard-edged sound of bebop, played by small groups like Dizzy Gillespie's, and the emphatic sound of Charlie Parker's alto sax and Miles Davis's trumpet. The mellow tones of Bing Crosby were being replaced by the youthful energy of Frank Sinatra, whose singing made bobby-soxers scream and cry. The new music was the sound of the new generation, strong, forceful, committed and intolerant of middle-class established society.

The relaxing of moral codes during wartime had made sexual intimacy an unquestioned part of the pattern of male-female relationships. Condoms and other protective devices, along with penicillin and antibiotics, had reduced the fear of unwanted pregnancies and sexual disease. Frank relationships were much more acceptable. Here, too, it was an American who led the way; the sexologist Alfred Kinsey's Sexual

BELOW: *CHILDREN QUEUE FOR THE CINEMA, 1945*
The children queuing outside this cinema for a Saturday morning show enjoyed a new form of entertainment which was exciting and educational and gave their parents time to go shopping ❧

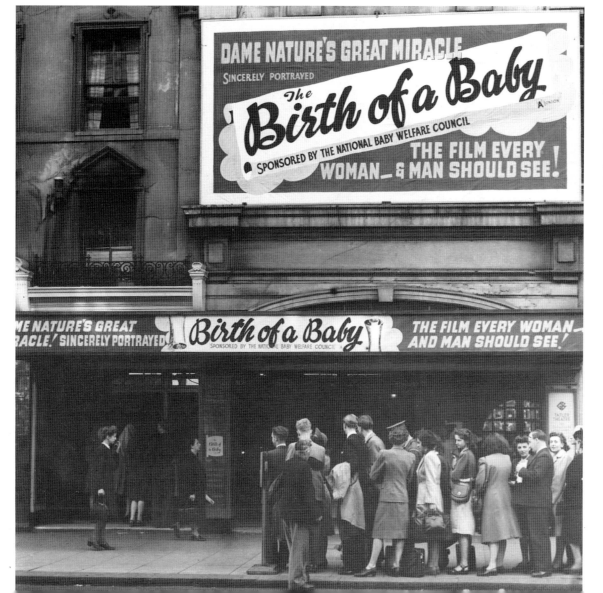

LEFT: *EXTERIOR OF CINEMA*
Adults queuing outside this cinema probably had little idea about human biology, even if they were parents, but a growing interest in the science of human life guaranteed an audience for a film entitled The Birth of a Baby

BELOW: *CROSSING THE ROAD TOGETHER*
These typical ragamuffins of a Glasgow slum in 1948 had few opportunities to become educated but the post war years brought many changes in the education and health of the whole population ❧

Behaviour in the Human Male and other books helped form new attitudes to sexual behaviour.

Women's magazine publishing moved ahead by leaps and bounds after wartime restrictions on printing and paper were relaxed. While these magazines fostered a romantic image for women, bolstered by advertisements for cosmetics and perfumes, they also included among the knitting patterns and cookery recipes much writing about sexual matters and how to give and receive pleasure. There was also an increase in the numbers of magazines for men published, with publications like *Men Only* and *Lilliput* adopting a more sophisticated tone which flattered their readers.

Cinema-going became an increasingly popular pastime in the late 1940s. While families went to the cinema regularly, it was among the young that going to the pictures was particularly popular. In contrast to much of the output of British film studios, American films created a new life-style, and there was a cult of imitation of the stars of the silver screen, in fashions, hair-styles and language. Cinemas, built to imitate Egyptian temples, Spanish haciendas or Mexican villas, were places where everyone could escape into a glamorous world of romance and adventure and forget for a while the aggravations of the real world of ration books, work and the domestic discomforts of shattered cities. Clark Gable, Gary Cooper, and the like became prototypes of the ideal male and Greer Garson and Ginger Rogers models of female personality.

There were, of course, plenty of home-grown, essentially British expressions of attitudes in the post-war years. Improvements in education had increased the interest in books and other aspects of culture that swung between the poles of post-war optimism and pessimism, hope and scepticism. George Orwell took a hard look at life and came up with *Animal Farm*, published in 1945 and *1984* (1949), both of which took pessimistic views of life in Britain and which were also warnings about the dangers of conventional rationalist thought. Graham Green wrote *The Heart of the Matter*, a novel exploring a love affair, and

BELOW: *CYCLISTS ON TANDEMS, 1948*
With little competition from automobiles
cycling club members were able to enjoy
safe outings with the whole family at low
cost ❦

Winston Churchill began producing a series of best-selling histories of Britain and her Empire.

The ferment of opinions and ideas of the time helped create a new British culture that would flourish in the second half of the century, a period when there would also be a smooth and relatively trouble-free transformation of Britain from the head of a world-wide empire to a democratic community whose head of state was also head of a Commonwealth of equal partners. British culture would soon lead the world in art, fashion, design and music while the country was becoming a major player in the worlds of finance, insurance and service industries.

LEFT: *STREET IN THE GORBALS*
The Gorbals were famous throughout Britain in 1948 as the toughest quarter of Glasgow, where out of work dock workers met and foreigners from over the border were not particularly welcome ❧

BELOW: *KILLING TIME BEFORE A CRICKET MATCH*
The great national game also popular in Australia, New Zealand, South Africa, India, Sri-Lanka and The West Indies, had always attracted the young, some of whom are seen here as they wait for the gates of the Oval to open in 1948 ❧

Memories Saved Forever

The arrival of a cheap camera, easy to manage and able to take clear pictures, enabled the public to record family life and special events to show friends and to keep as reminders of happy occasions.

At first, the photographs were in black and white but by the 1930s colour film was available and, soon after, colour print film. These were carefully preserved in albums or enlarged and framed when required.

LEFT: *THE FUNERAL OF QUEEN VICTORIA*
Britain's longest-reigning monarch, Queen Victoria, died peacefully at Osborne House on the Isle of Wight on 22 January, 1901, aged 81. Here can be seen the funeral cortège on its way to St George's Chapel, in the precincts of Windsor Castle, on 2 February, 1901 ℥

RIGHT: *PARK BENCH FOR TWO*
Two-person benches installed in London Parks, like this one in Battersea in 1948, were much appreciated by couples and avoided grass stains on clothes ℥

ABOVE: "KODAK GIRL" POSING WITH CAMERA, 1909
*The Kodak folding camera was an improvement on the old box Brownie
and could be focused and the light controlled by a shutter on the lens* ❧

ABOVE: CHRISTENING OF PRINCESS ANNE
*Princess Elizabeth, who became queen on her father's death in 1952, is seen
here with her daughter Anne, after her christening at Buckingham Palace in 1950* ❧

The first popular and easily managed camera was the Kodak Box Brownie, which was a development of the camera obscura, a device used since the eighteenth century, allowing light through a pinhole to project an outside image onto the inner wall of a box, upside-down. The simple Kodak Box Brownie soon became more complicated with lenses controlling the strength of the light and bellows to move the lens backwards and forwards for focus. There was also a camera, called Polaroid Land which delivered a colour print within a few minutes. Then came a hand held movie camera which brought active scenes into a living room on 8 or 9 mm film. The new technical developments increased public interest in photography and recorded memories in a way that had once been the province of artists.

Though the new medium had commercial uses, the greatest area of its use was by individuals and families, who now kept a visual record of children, adults and shared family activities like weddings, christenings, funerals, school events, holidays etc, as

BELOW: *HENRY FARMAN MAKES FIRST CIRCULAR FLIGHT, JANUARY 1908*
Henry Farman flew at Issyles-Mouineaus in the Voisin Biplane that he designed himself ⚙

well as scenes from local life. This created a whole new industry for film manufacturers like Kodak, Agfa and laboratories which processed the films.

The preservation of memories was also the province of the movie industry which produced news reels, documentaries and films with popular themes. Audiences saw in the dramas a reflection of their own lives and were prone to identifying themselves, friends or relatives with the actors on the screen. This had a powerful effect on the manners and dress of the public, who modelled themselves on the screen personalities and filled offices with 'look alike' Clark Gables or Gary Coopers and 'would be' blonde bombshells like Jean Harlow, or redheads such as Rita Hayworth.

RIGHT: *KING KONG POSTER*
Epic films were an American speciality and King Kong, the story of a giant ape machine gunned to death by aircraft on the Empire State building was an instant success in London at the Coliseum Theatre, 1933

LEFT: *THE TITANIC*
On April 10, 1912, the
RMS Titanic *set sail*
from Southampton on
her maiden voyage to
New York. At that time,
she was the largest and
most luxurious ship
ever built. At 11:40 p.m.
on April 14, 1912, she
struck an iceberg about
400 miles off
Newfoundland,
Canada ❧

ABOVE: *FLOOD VICTIMS RECEIVE HELP*
A flood in Wales was only one problem in the declining prosperity of the valleys of the coal industry of the 1930s. During a visit the Prince of Wales had declared that 'something must be done', and here the Salvation Army are giving practical aid with free soup and bread ❧

LEFT: *PEDLAR IN LONDON*
During the Depression of the 1930s many people took to hawking products they could not sell through the shops. Here a street pedlar is offering a housewife some fresh meat cuts ❧

RIGHT: *SHEEP ON PARK LANE, LONDON, 1930*
An unusual sight was this flock of 600 sheep which had been feeding in Hyde Park, being driven down to Green Park for a further meal before, one assumes, being sent to the slaughterhouse

LEFT: *SCOTT DISCOVERS AMUNDSEN'S TENT*
Robert Falcon Scott (1868–1912) was a British naval officer and Antartic explorer. Scott led two expeditions to the South Pole, and died on the disastrous second trip, along with his crew. His expedition was the second to reach the South Pole (1910–1912). Roald Amundsen led the first. This picture shows Scott discovering Amundsen's tent when he arrived at the South Pole ❧

RIGHT: *MARCH OF THE UNEMPLOYED*
The Great Depression of the 1930s aroused much anger and bitterness among working people but there was no violence, as in other countries. Instead the patient British workmen marched to London in large numbers and were eventually listened to ❧

The copycat effect sometimes lasted for years, even after the stars on whom they were based had faded, but was a form of preservation of memories and of an identity.

Not all memories were happy ones, however, and some of the films made in the 1930s were reminders of the horrors of war and reflected a powerful anti-war feeling among many members of the public, who later supported appeasement policies in dealing with Hitler. These films included *All Quiet On The Western Front*, an American film starring Lew Ayres and the Marx brothers in *Duck Soup* which satirised the supidity and futility of war.

Music also preserved memories, sometimes for a lifetime in such songs as *These Foolish Things* which recalled small but important items of listeners lives in lyrics such as as: *The cigarette that bears a lipsticks traces, an airline ticket to romantic places.* The musical sentimental memories were preserved on ten inch or long playing discs and made millionaires of singers like Bing Crosby and Frank Sinatra. A minor form of memory preservation was, and still is,

the souvenir object such as mugs or plates to commemorate royal jubilees, and items like colour postcards, cheap jewellery etc, that are brought back from visits to the seaside or foreign resorts. All these are landmarks of memory, like photographs, film and music which became available to the general public in the first half of the twentieth century and will continue to revive happy memories in the future.

The inclination to collect memories was the result of the growth of public education, for in the days of the illiterate poor nobody had the time or the money for collecting and the wealthier classes wrapped in their private worlds were not interested. The growth of the educated middle classes increased the interest in the behaviour and appearance of other people – to confirm their uniformity or to criticise their idiosyncracies.

ABOVE: *PARCEL WAGON*
Deliveries by horse drawn wagons were still in operation in the early 1930s, as this picture shows. One of the largest delivery companies was Carter Paterson

LEFT: *FAMILY CELEBRATIONS, VE DAY May 1945, was celebrated all over Britain in a most heartfelt way, for never before had a whole nation been in the front line and suffered so much destruction* ❧

BELOW: *FIRST WOMAN TO FLY SOLO Amy Johnson set off alone in a single engine Gypsy Moth from Croydon on May 5, 1930, and landed in Darwin, Australia, on May 24, an epic flight of 11,000 miles. She was the first woman to fly alone to Australia* ❧

LEFT: *DELIVERING MILK TO BOMBED STREET, 1940*
A milkman at his daily round had to walk through piles of rubble but his service was invaluable to older people and those unable to get to the shops ❧

FAR LEFT: *BOYS SORTING SHRAPNEL*
During lulls in the air raids, boys would go out into the streets to collect interestingly shaped bits of shrapnel, seemingly unaware of their deadly significance ❧

Middle-classness was a form of identity for individuals who had come together in the new acres of suburbia around large cities and everyone strove to remain within the parameters of acceptable beliefs and behaviour. By the mid twentieth century and after two world wars, the walls of the edifice of national opinion were crumbling and memories began to become less important than the realities of everyday living.

RIGHT: *THE QUEEN MARY*
The Queen Mary, one of the largest Atlantic liners, was launched on September 26, 1934, by HM Queen Mary. It was a day of great excitement. Throngs of spectators lined the shores of the river Clyde to witness the birth of one of Britain's greatest achievements ⚓

FAR RIGHT: *BREAKING THE LAND SPEED RECORD*
On Febuary 4, 1927, Donald Campbell drove the Napier-Campbell Bluebird to 174.883 mph (281.447 kph) on the beach at Pendine. The Bluebird was the first car built specifically for breaking the land speed record. Here a crowd of school children gather round the Bluebird in awe at the fastest piloted car in the world ⚓

ABOVE: *CHILDREN WITH RECORD PLAYER*
For young boys of different cultures from the polyglot dockland area of Cardiff, there was a fascination for Rock music, it is hardly suprising as they listen to a ten inch record ℘

LEFT: *VALVE FOR TELEPHONE SERVICE*
One of the 33 valves which was used for transmitting the London to New York wireless telephone service in 1930 was a wonder of its age, as one can verify by the expression on the face of the Postmaster General in this photo ℘

LEFT: *THE SPITFIRE*
A squadron of British Spitfire 8-gun monoplane fighters in flight over London in 1939. Also called the Supermarine Spitfire, it was the most widely-produced and strategically important British single-seat fighter of World War II. The Spitfire is renowned for winning victory laurels in the Battle of Britain (1940–41) ✥

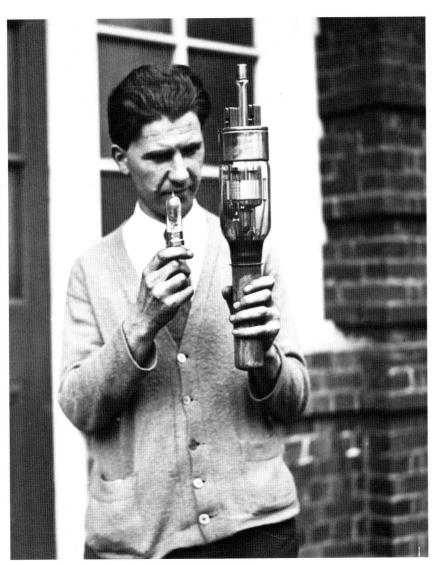

ABOVE: *CHILDREN WITH RECORD PLAYER*
For young boys of different cultures from the polyglot dockland area of Cardiff, there was a fascination for Rock music, it is hardly suprising as they listen to a ten inch record ⬧

LEFT: *VALVE FOR TELEPHONE SERVICE*
One of the 33 valves which was used for transmitting the London to New York wireless telephone service in 1930 was a wonder of its age, as one can verify by the expression on the face of the Postmaster General in this photo ⬧

LEFT: *THE SPITFIRE*
A squadron of British Spitfire 8-gun monoplane fighters in flight over London in 1939. Also called the Supermarine Spitfire, it was the most widely-produced and strategically important British single-seat fighter of World War II. The Spitfire is renowned for winning victory laurels in the Battle of Britain (1940–41)